Alligators,
Monsters &
S
cool
h
o
Poems
l

Author:
Addie Meyer Sanders
Illustrator: Dave Sanders Jr.

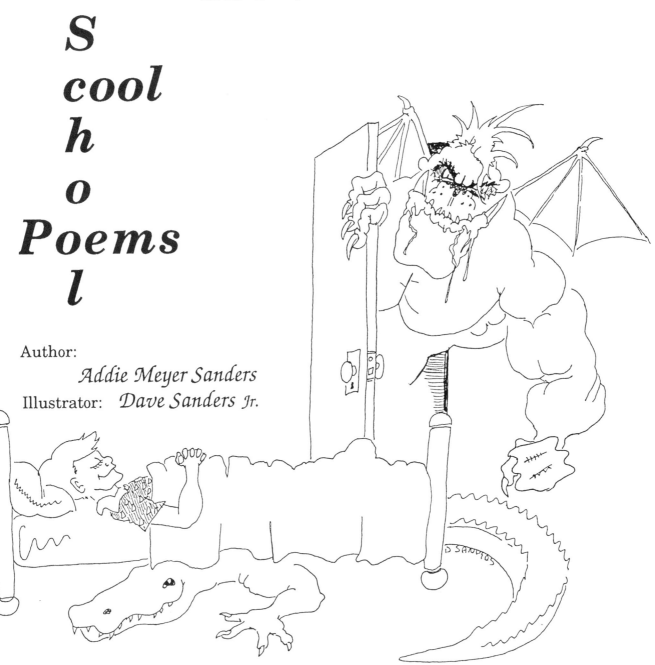

This is a g-r-o-w-i-n-g book.
Add your own ideas.

About the Author and Illustrator:

About the Author...

Addie (Adelaide) Meyer Sanders was born in Brooklyn and grew up in Baldwin, Long Island, New York. She was graduated from the State University of New York at Oneonta with a Bachelor of Science Degree in Elementary Education and permanent teaching certification. In 1989, Addie earned a Master of Arts Degree in Secondary Education-English at Hofstra University. Addie visits schools conducting student writing workshops and teacher in-service seminars.

About the illustrator....

Dave Sanders Jr. grew up in Sayville, Long Island, New York. He captained the high school football team and received many honors for his art work. Dave was graduated from the State University of New York at Cortland with a Bachelor of Science Degree in Management Science while helping the Rugby Team acquire Four State Championships. He plans a career in business management.

More books by the author....

THE UPSIDE-DOWN KIDS; Helping Dyslexic Children Understand Themselves and Their Disorder by Harold Levinson, M.D. and Addie Sanders, M.A. Evans Publishing, NYC. A story that offers new hope and a helping hand to all dyslexic children, their families and concerned professionals.

TURNING AROUND THE UPSIDE-DOWN KIDS, Levinson & Sanders. A story showing the latest educational, technical and medical methods that may be used to help students learn.

Author:
Addie Meyer Sanders
Illustrator: *Dave Sanders Jr.*

Table of Contents

Text: © Addie Meyer Sanders, 1995   Graphics: © Dave Sanders, Jr., 1995

"G-r-o-w-i-n-g books" is a line of books exclusive to Leadership Publishers Inc.
ISBN: 0-911943-45-5

Leadership Publishers Inc.
Promoting Leadership & Human Potential
P.O. Box 8358
Des Moines, Iowa 50301

This book is dedicated to

DAVE

for his love, faith and support

KRISTIN - DAVID - KARRIN

and to
all the poets
in my writing workshops

and all others who try.

First Day

Today's the first day of school.
I don't think I can go.
My stomach is a baseball.
My heart's about to blow.

My mouth is like a desert.
My eyes are blurry - bright.
My ears hear all things fuzzy.
I didn't sleep last night.

My shoe's untied.
Dirt's on my shirt.
My hair's a mess.
My big toe hurts.

Hands hiding deep in my pants.
Will pockets stop the shake?
I wish I was just dreaming.
But nope! I am awake.

Oh, no, here comes a new kid.
Bet he's not scared like me.
He walks up and whispers, "Hi."
And suddenly I see.

HIS hands are in his pockets.
Dirt's on his shirt and knee.
Yes! His hands are hidden deep.
"Hi, friend," You're just like me!"

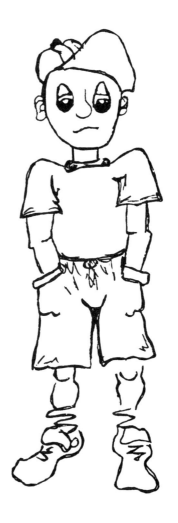

Scary School Sounds

Serpents in the radiator
    Make a hiss and clunk.
The gruber-monster in Tom's desk
    Keeps it full of junk.

The squeaky seat of Leslie Ray.
    The dropped ball from Phil.
Makes us giggle, want to play. No!
    More dittos to fill.

A sneeze, a laugh, a groan, a croak.
    Takes our minds away.
Out in the sun, come on, play ball,
    Please, don't make us stay.

Then suddenly, a sick sound squeals.
    Chills race down our spines.
Fingernails scrape on the chalk-board.

    Sorry kids, they're mine!

Sea Shell Songs

I found sea shells at the shore.
   Everyday I searched for more.
Some were silver, white and blue.
   Yellow and orange - I could see through.

Round ones, long ones - smooth or rough,
   Some were fragile, some were tough.
Big ones held against my ear,
   Sang the ocean song all year.

If you want to hear it too,
   This is all you have to do.
You don't need a shell or gear,
   Just cup your hand over your ear!

Trick or Treat

It's Halloween.
I'm going out
and I'm not scared at all.

The street is black.
Long shadows move, branches moan,
Cats meow...
And I'm not scared at all.

The house is dark
But in the window the
Crooked smile of the
Jack-o-lantern flickers....
And I'm not scared at all.

I knock.
 S l o w l y
C r e a k i n g
The door opens. A hand
Reaches out. I yell ... Hi Mom!
And I'm not scared at all.

4

Haunted Houses

Haunted houses
Haunted houses
Ghosts and SQUEALS
and HOWLS.

Haunted houses
Haunted houses
Books fly off
The shelves.

Haunted houses
Haunted houses
Meet the FRIENDLY
WITCH!

Haunted houses
Haunted houses
Watch out for
A TRICK!

Pep Rally

Everyone gathers
In the gym.
The band plays loud
Marching songs.
Cheerleaders and
Pom poms jump
Up and down.
The team arrives
Like conquering heroes.
Cheers shake and rattle
The roof and tomorrow's
Victory is almost
Here.

The Quarterback No One Knew

Walking. Unsteady. His left foot
Leaves a narrow trail. Arms limp.
Mouth hangs. Glassy eyes stare
Until .... FOOTBALL SEASON.

Life and sparkle excite
A dead face in a deformed body. Year
After year - animation, joy, delight
Come in thick slurred syllables announcing

His team. His heroes. Perfectly fit
Players of a team he can never join.
A new season. Pep rally. Cheers.
Beautiful girls. Masses of purple

Shirts with huge gold numbers. Suddenly,
They call his name. Admidst cheers and
Tears he lumbers on stage. For him ...
A purple shirt with huge gold numbers,
        and HIS name on it.

Love

Love is good.
Love you will find.
If you love yourself.
You'll love mankind.

Just Me

I am good.
    I am a gift.
Just the way I am.

And everyday
    In everyway
I carry out God's plan.

God's Name

God's name is Harold.
    Tim shouted with glee.
I heard it on Sunday.
    When down on my knee.

The preacher said it.
    It wasn't a game.
"Our Father who art in heaven,
    'Harold' be thy name."

Secret Place

Behind the couch
      Where no one can see.
That is the place
      I like to hide me.
I'll read a story
      Or maybe a poem.
I'll be a King. A Queen!
      The Emperor of Rome.
I'm never alone.
      I'm not mad or sad.
I giggle and laugh and
      Feel really glad.
But sometimes a story
      May make me cry.
Especially if the King
      Or the Queen should die.
But to make them live
      And be happy again,
I'll write my own story.
      Hey! Where's my pen?

Tests

Spelling test
Spelling test
    Just watch me.
    I studied my words.
    I'll get a hundred.
        Oops!

Math test
Math test
    Easy as 1-2-3
    I studied my numbers.
    I'll get a hundred.
        Oops!

Science test
Science test
    Electricity and light.
    I studied all night.
    I'll get a hundred.
        Oops!

Tests
Tests
  Too many tests.
  But I know next week,
  I'll get a hundred.
        Next week!

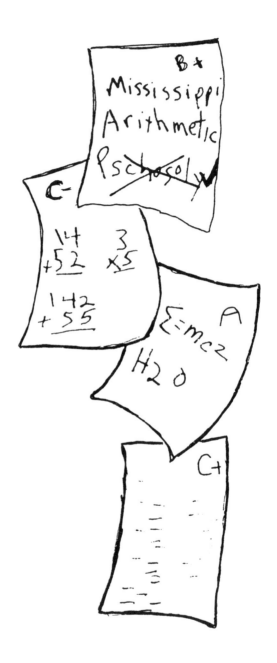

School Lunch

I forget my lunch.
  What'll I do?
I'll have to eat food.
  At the school zoo.

Maybe it's liver?
  Or fried fish tails?
Lizard eyes, octopus?
  Or slimy snails?

What's a kid to do?
  Just wait and pray.
YES! YES! YES! YES! YES!
  It's PIZZA day.

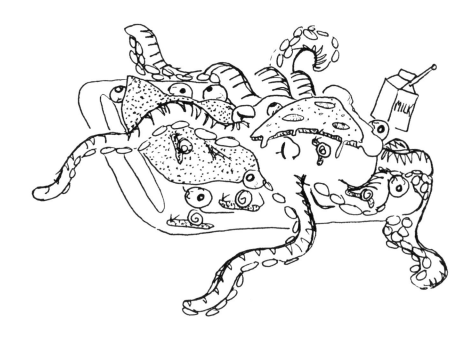

The Terrible Zoor

Oh, no, here he comes
The terrible Zoor
Flying in through the window
And locking the door.

Zoor ate all the books
Papers, pencils and pens.
He erased all the hundreds
and eighties and tens.

Zoor broke up the desks
And crumbled the chairs.
He threw all the chalkboards
Crashing down the stairs.

Zoor ate up the teacher
And then with a grin
He ate up the principal
He's going to win.

Zoor stared at us kids
His evil eyes red ....
Wake up, Tom. Good news.
You can stay in bed.

School's closed. Too much snow.
The sign's on the door.
Tom looked at the window. Ha!
He knew it was ZOOR.

13

Guess the Animal

If I Were A _____.

I'd see
    stormy skies and salty
    white water washing
    along the soft sand.

I'd hear
    wild waves crashing
    people laughing
    kids splashing.

I'd eat
    fat smelly fish
    clammy clams and
    gloppy gooey garbage.

A bad day
    would be if I were tossed
    in a wave or found
    no food or friends.

A good day
    would be if I found five
    fine feathered friends
    to go flying with.

I would feel like a
    jet plane soaring
    a rocket diving and a
    white cloud drifting by.

(Answer: seagull)

Best Lunch Box Treat

In Mary's lunch box
    she found tuna fish.
Tommy had macaroni
    sealed in a dish.
Anna ate applesauce
    from a jar.
Benny brought a chewy, gooey,
    chocolate bar.
But Melanie's lunch was best
    by far.
Better than
    a candy bar.
Everyone waited for the
    special note.
Sometimes a love
    poem.
Sometimes a
    joke
That her Dad tucked in
    her lunch each day.
Everyone waited to hear
    what he's say.
They'd giggle and laugh
    and they knew why.
Melanie's lunch
    beat one you could buy.

Recess

Randy is a
  dragon.
There's fire in
  his eyes.
He's racing across
  the field.
Don't get in his way
  HURRY...
Randy's racing across
  the field.
There's fire in
  his eyes.

Randy is a
  dragon
At recess.

After School Today

After school today
I think I'll take a
Rocket ship to Mars.

After school today
I think I'll become a bird
And fly far away and
Never ever come back

After school today
I think I will
Take a s l o w
Boat to China.

After School today
I have
    To go
        To the dentist!!!

17

Too Many Nicks

There are too many Nicks in class.
I wonder if all Nicks will pass?
There's a Nick on the floor.
There's a Nick by the door.
There are too many Nicks in class.

There are too many Nicks in class.
A few are lads, others a lass.
There's a Nick in the back.
There's a Nick having a snack.
There are too many Nicks in class.

So what is a teacher to do?
When she calls out "Nick!" here comes two.
Or three or maybe four,
Yes, sometimes, even more!
"No, not YOU!" she yells 'til she's blue.

There are too many Nicks in class.
Yes, I'm sure every Nick will pass.
When one Nick gets an "A",
All the Nicks shout, "Hurray!"
It's great being a Nick in this class!

Text: © Addie Meyers Sanders, 1995   Illustrations: © Dave Sanders Jr., 1995

Not Fair

My puppy likes
   to sleep on my bed.
But he's so big
   and fat.
That when he goes
   to sleep on my bed,
I have to sleep on
   his mat!

Gym Class

Today I'll do the flip in gym.
I promised myself I would.
I tried it first in second grade.
I really thought I could.

But my hand slipped. I fell. I tried
Again. It just wouldn't work.
I tried it over in third grade.
I missed. It really hurt.

The bar so high. I had to fly.
I knew I'd do it one day.
But when the fourth grade came, and went.
I didn't know what to say.

Finally in fifth, with sweat on
Brow, my eyes stared at that
Bar. Silence. I ran. I jumped. I
Flipped. I really did go far.

Up and over. Around and down.
I FINALLY MADE THE FLIP.
I didn't even care at all,
When I heard my gym shorts *riiiip!*

I'm Smart

I'm smart. I can.
I'm smart. I can.
Feed myself.
Get dressed.
Sing a song.

I'm smart. I can.
I'm smart. I can.
Read a book.
Write a story.
Learn a poem.

I'm smart. I can.
I'm smart. I can.
Add. Subtract.
Multiply. Divide.

I'm smart. I can.
I'm smart. I can.
Do all the things
I used to think I
Thought I couldn't do.

But now I know.
I'm smart! I can!

21

Cool School
(A Rap Poem)

We have a sub
Great day in school.
Let's all sit back
And be real cool.

> Johnny and Sam
> Quickly changed seats.
> Patty and Pam
> Tripped over feet.

Eli, Allen
Agatha, Ted
Changed seats fast - Yikes!
They will be dead.

> They weren't caught.
> Her head was down.
> Mary and Sue
> Moved clear 'cross town.

Mark and Mandy
Switched seats fast, Bob
Bill, Betty, Ben ....
They were the last.

> Then Ms. Slick smiled
> Called Johnny - Sam.
> We thought we'd die....
> Patty was Pam.

Allen, Eli -
Didn't laugh or
Joke...Ag was Ted
Choke, choke, choke, choke!

> And nobody
> Told poor Ms. Slick
> She just played
> Along with the trick.

So let me say
When you're in school
And have a sub
Just be real cool.

Text: © Addie Meyers Sanders, 1995   Illustrations: © Dave Sanders Jr., 1995

Dudley

Dudley's in the classroom.
He's over by the sink.
No one ever sees him.
But you can hear him clink.

Dudley never does his work.
Never opens up a book.
Makes a ruckus and racket.
Get's a teacher's dirty look.

When the class is quiet.
So softly from the wall.
Dudley starts his hissing.
Hissssssing LOUDLY is his call.

Clinks and clanks and clunks and
BANGS!   His rattles rock the room.
DUDLEY!   screams the teacher.
Oops. Ssssh That's Dudley's doom.

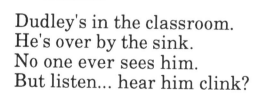

Dudley's in the classroom.
He's over by the sink.
No one ever sees him.
But listen... hear him clink?

Daydreams

The boy in the back row

sat

and stared

out

the window

watching

the bird

on the branch

fly

free.

Immigrants

The waters opened
The sky's azure blue
They forget the troubles
They all had been through.

Trails strewn with bodies
The sick, weak and lame
Price paid for the promise
Joy. Anxiety. Pain.

Clasping a child's hand
Clinging to a love
Boat lists - all rush to see
THE LADY - Liberty - above.

New York Harbor
Sailed right past
Ellis Island
Here at last.

Name? Country?
Eyes? Teeth?
So many languages
So much to meet.

Papers marked
Finally on their way
Shoulders back - head held high
America! Here to stay.

A hundred years
Since they sailed to our shore
Ancestors hear your children say
Your courage makes us shudder in awe.

Tonsil Time

Two boys were discussing
    Their hospital stay.
IT WAS GROSS! MY BIKE CRASHED!
    I BLED ALL THE WAY.

NOT ME, said the other.
    IT SEEMED LIKE A DREAM.
FOR A WEEK ALL I ATE
    WAS CHOCOLATE ICE CREAM!

A Special Friend

Ian has an
Invisible friend.
He sleeps with Ian
But always keeps one
Eye open - to be a good guard.
There is a plate set for
Him at the table, next to Ian.
He especially likes seconds
In dessert, but will only eat
After the family is finished.
He rides double on Ian's bike and
They swing like monkeys in the trees.
He hates playing baseball where
He swings and misses but
He likes school because
He never has to answer a question or
Read out loud, or spell or
Add, subtract, multiply or divide.
He never fails a test because
He never has to take one.
He's really cool. Not crazy
Running around and getting in trouble.
He makes Ian feel really cool, too, and
He will stay and play with Ian for as
Long as Ian wants him to be his own
Very special fun invisible friend.

Text: © Addie Meyers Sanders, 1995   Illustrations: © Dave Sanders Jr., 1995

If

*(May be said standing
using arm movements)*

If I were a bird
I'd wonder why
All animals never
learned to fly.

If I were a giraffe
I'd hope by heck
I'd never get
A pain in the neck.

If I were a house
I'd always be
Cozy and warm
For those who lived in me.

If I were a tree
I'd stand straight and tall
And never let
A girl or boy fall.

If I were a fish
And lived in the sea
I'd never, NO NEVER,
Let someone catch me.

If I were a bat
I'd giggle with glee
When people S C R E A M E D
And ran from me.

If I were a dog, I'd chase
a cat. If I were a cat
I'd climb a tree. Especially
if that dog was after me!

But I am me
And I'm happy you see
Because I can dream
What I want to be.

Dazzling Dinosaurs

Allosaurus, Ankylosaurus,
Stegosaurus, too.
Dimetrodon and Pteranodon
Never at the zoo.

Three toes on front feet, sledgehammer tail,
Tall plates on the back,
Frightening top-sail, wide wings that fly -
Match the name to fact?

Sydney

Sydney
is so silly and
he always makes a mess
and then I get in trouble....

because he's my baby brother!

Funny Feelings

Sometimes I feel dumb.
Sometimes I feel *ug-l- y.*
But when somebody yells, *"GREAT!"*
Suddenly I feel cuddly!

31

Believing

Softly, silently
teeny, tiny tip toes
race across
cold wooden floors.

Pitch black midnight hour
frosted stars fill the sky
path lit by
milk-white moon dust.

Bouncing, bending, peek
through stair slats - eyes expand
dance with delight
colored bulbs glow.

Red, orange, yellow
against a sea of green
packages
mounds of ice cream.

Gasp is muffled, a
black boot seen - footprints in
ashes - NO!
he left his glasses!

Softly, silently
tip toe back to bed-yes!
believing
excited eyes close.

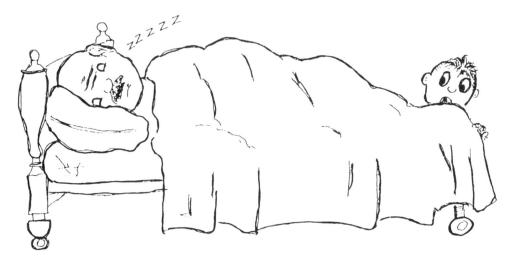

Happy New Year

This year
      I will
Be nice to my brother
      Share with my sister
Do what I'm told
      Clean up my room
Not hide snakes and bugs
      Under my bed (makes mom mad)
Eat all my vegetables
      With my mouth closed
(But I still don't see
      How I'll breathe)
Keep my elbows off the table
      Do my homework
On time
      Not talk out in class
Or push. Or shove
      Or pull Amy's hair
Or....WAIT! This year
      I will just rip
Up the list of things
      To do*RRRIIIIIPPPPP!*
And maybe I'll just be
      A better bestest me.

11:38 am

January 28, 1986

white smoke bubbled along the earth
engines fired - liftoff
slowly space shuttle leaves launch pad
cheers!
six astronauts - one teacher
aloft

BOOM

billows of smoke - monstrous flames
two jets zig-jag
uncontrollably, going nowhere.
open-mouthed .... silence.

a nation mourns her heroes
those who taught the best lessons of all
reach for the stars
excel - work hard
believe in the impossible
test the challenge
encounter the adventure
live with enthusiasm, zest and
courage
right to the end
six astronauts - one teacher
aloft.

A Limerick

I once saw a dolphin at sea
Tail walking and whistling at me
   He jumped high in the air
   Water splashed everywhere
Then I was as salty as he.

Ski ing

I went
skiing once.
I stood
on the
top of
the hill
then I
started to
slide down
faster faster
faster my
until spread
feet and
farther apart
farther I
so

sat.

The Silver Locket

The silver locket laced with
    tiny engraved flowers, hangs heavy
    on a shiny black string.
The locket was first worn by a lady
    on a long trip that carried
    her over the seas from the
    old world to the new.
The locket, laying close to her
    heart, held a picture of her love.
    Later she gave the locket to her
    daughter in New York, who added to
The locket her love. Many long years
    later she gave the locket to
    her daughter on Long Island who
    added to the locket her love. She wore
The locket close to her heart
    and knew that the locket
    of loves helped her to know
    the lady she never knew.

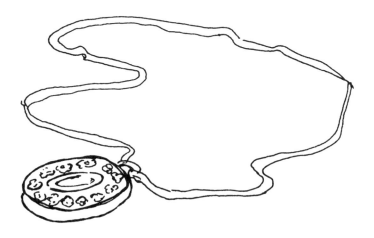

The Green Kid in Class

The green kid in class
Never
Takes a test or
Does math or
 spelling or
 science or
 social studies or
 even gym.
The green kid in class
Never
Has to wash hands
Clean his corner
 raise his hand
 be quiet
 say please or
 thank you.
The green kid in class
Just sits
In his corner
And grins his
 wide green
 ugly iguana grin
 while he watches
 us work.

Spring Rain

Through the raindrops
    wishing, washing
Looms the land of
    slush and sloshing.
In your ears sounds
    softly slurred
In your eyes your
    visions blurred.
Slowly, coldly
    down your back
Raindrop rivers
    trail a track.
Squirmy puddles
    deep and dark
Take your aim
    make your mark.

In the center
    world's divide
Muddy water
    slip, slide.
Soaking, swimming
    splish, splash
Happy in your first
    Spring bath.

Imagination

I s in all humans

M akes creativity marvelous

A nd all things possible.

G reat power to get to goals.

I am. I can. I will dream

N ew dreams

A nd

T urn people on by

I nventing, inspiring, igniting ideas

O n this planet that will make minds soar towards

N arnia and places beyond beginnings.

Presidents

George and Abe
Great Presidents, true.
And who knows?
The next could be YOU!

Home Sweet Home

There's no place like home.
There's no place like home.
With a remote control in one hand
And in the other hand .... a phone.

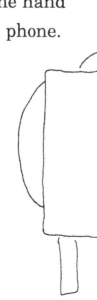

41

Mr. Shoulda

i shoulda studied harder
for the social studies test.
i shoulda not lost my school bag
with my reading book in
it and my pencil case and
my eraser. i shoulda
not left my coat at the movies
or let my scarf, that nanna knit
me, blow away in the breeze. i
shoulda found my other sneaker
for gym but i couldn't and
i shoulda not tripped in gym class
or dropped the ball out on the
field during the game. i shoulda
been more careful in art and
not knocked over the bucket of
black paint or left the glue on
the teacher's seat. i shoulda not
burped in class or dropped my crazy
crayons all over the floor. i
shoulda listened when i talked,
i shoulda walked when i ran
down the hall and bumped smack into
the principal's broad back. i shoulda
woulda coulda done a lot of things
i know, but sometimes Mr. Shoulda
never lets me go and do the
things i know i shoulda woulda
coulda done if Mr. Shoulda
woulda let me.

Quiet Time

There's a monster in my closet
Alligators under the bed
Vampire bats hit my window
At night when I put down my head.

Wild tigers fill the TV room
The bath bubbles with babbling bears
Wolves howl and whistle with the wind
But all's peace when I say my prayers.

43

Cinquains

Cinquains
Syllables or
Counted words on a line
Five lines, just 2, 4, 6, 8, 2
A poem.

Poet writers
Blake, Brooks, Browning, Dickinson,
Eliot, Frost, Hughes, Lowell, Millay, Milne,
Nash, Poe, Sandburg, Seuss, Silverstein, Whitman, Yeats give
Words life.

MUSIC

Magic melodies
Move the mind's spirit
Moments making goose bumps fill flesh
Together riding waves in ocean of my imagination
Soaring.   Exploring.

Haikus

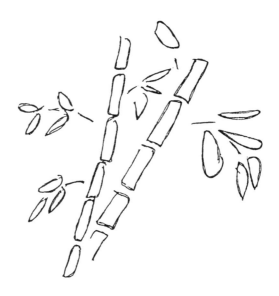

S U M M E R

Blue, pink, yellow, gold
Happy splashes bright and bold
Shouts. Laughs. Cricket songs.

A U T U M N

Blood red maple leaf
Drifts softly through morning mist
Final curtain call.

W I N T E R

White crystal curtain
Masking the face of the earth
Hiding its life pulse.

S P R I N G

Gray sheets of warm rain
Green grass, flowers, buds pop-out
Welcome back old friends.

Moved

New girl in class
     she cried
From India
     she cried
Can't speak English
     she cried.

If I moved away
     I'd cry.
So I touched her hand
     she smiled
She held my hand
     we smiled.
       MOVED.

A Rainbow of Eggs

The Easter Egg hunt begins,
    I have my basket ready.
I want to find colored eggs.
    Oh, no, here's pushy Freddy.

He grabs one egg, then two and
    three and four and five and more.
But wait I see a red one
    and an orange by the door.

Here's a yellow like the sun
    and a green as sweet as grass.
Look at this blue, like summer
    skies, I didn't let it pass.

And far away, under a bush,
I spy the best by far.
I give the leaf a gentle push,
YES! This one has the star.

Royal purple fills my hand
soft as a lullaby.
When I place it with the rest,
a RAINBOW fills the sky.

Flag Day

When I Salute Our

A merican flag I see
M ighty mountains, majesties
E agles soaring in clear skies
R ed, white, and blue stripes flying
I ndian songs in whispering winds
C owboys riding the range and
A ll people united as one.

Sailing

I
Went
Sailing out
On the bay. The
Wind picked up. The
Sail filled and shook.
Speeding on its side, the
Ship cut water. Wind walloped
My chest like a hammer.   Bending
Backwards, salt spray stung my eyes.
Filled my mouth. White knuckles held onto
The line for life .... Finally, we came about.
The boom crashed over, just missing my head. The
Old white and red sail rippled and shook out the last
Of the wind.   I took a d-e-e-p b-r-e-a-t-h and I
Can't
Wait
To go out again on my next
    Super sailing trip.

The Wait

Blackness filled the sky and only
a tiny strip of purple hung over the
horizon showing where day left. Waiting.
Will he come? Chin in palms. Elbows
on knees. Curled forward on stoop. Eyes
frozen down the road. Waiting. First
star twinkled. "Star light, star
bright, first star..." Waiting. Inside
dishes clink and heady smell of
sauerkraut lingers. Blare of TV light lends
eerie glow. Suddenly. Finally. The
sound. Soft as spring. Then louder. Louder.
A tingle. A jingle. Out of the dark
emerges a mountain of white. Lights smiling
ringing 'round the creamy cube. One huge
brown popsicle on a stick hides, almost but
not completely, the tiny door. Rush to the
curb. Fists wave frantically clutching
allowance. The grinning man in white, as
shiny as an angel, pops me to his seat so I
can ring the beautiful string of silver bells.
And then it happens. He opens the magical
door. A cloud of white frosty air descends on me
sending a shiver down my spine and as the first
mouth watering bite of toasted almond
melts on my lips, I know it's summer.

Always

Seek
    and you will find
Ask
    and you will be answered.
But how often do we
Seek
    without looking and
Ask
    without listening
So that we miss
Seeing
    and
Hearing
    and
Being refreshed.

51

Trip to the Beach

We went on a field trip

      to the

Beach

And I found

      seashells

Seaweed

      sand

Salt water

      a
      seahorse

    sand

Shark eggs

      and my

Salami

      sandwich

        filled

  with

SAND!

Vacation

V acation days are such fun.
A ll day long we laugh and run.
C atch me, catch me, if you can.
A t the beach we'll get a tan.
T rips. Company. Even camp. Sleep
I n the cold. Sleep in the damp.
O vernight away from home.
N o work, no school, no comb .... NO PHONE?

Help!

The purple sea surrounds me
    And turns my red lips blue.
My finger tips are white and shrunk
    I think I have the flu.

A silly serpent joins me
    He thinks this is his home
Then Mom pulls out the bath tub plug
    And all that's left is foam.

Keep a Journal

Take a book
Make it your own
Add a thought
An idea, a poem.

Tuck it away

Your secrets will keep

And when you're old

You just may weep.

With joy and laughs

At the things you did

When you were growing

When YOU were a kid.

The poet and artist have written & illustrated Part One.
From these writings & illustrations, the publisher created a book.
Part One of this book is ended.

The END
of this book is
the BEGINNING
of your book.

Part Two & Part Three are for _you!_

Part Two: The Illustrator is _you_. - pages 57-64.

Part Three: The Author is _you_. - pages 65-79

It's your turn to be the writer.
The rest of the book is for your journal
entries, illustrations, or whatever you
wish to include in this book.

Page 65 has some ideas for journal entries
- just in case you need ideas.

Part Two: pages 57-64

The

Illustrator

is

you!

Directions: Illustrate the poems on pages 57-64.

Secret Place

Behind the couch
     Where no one can see.
That is the place
     I like to hide me.
I'll read a story
     Or maybe a poem.
I'll be a King. A Queen!
     The Emperor of Rome.
I'm never alone.
     I'm not mad or sad.
I giggle and laugh and
     Feel really glad.
But sometimes a story
     May make me cry.
Especially if the King
     Or the Queen should die.
But to make them live
     And be happy again,
I'll write my own story.
     Hey! Where's my pen?

Text: © Addie Meyers Sanders, 1995

Illustrated by _____ *Date* _____

School Lunch

I forget my lunch.
    What'll I do?
I'll have to eat food.
    At the school zoo.

Maybe it's liver?
    Or fried fish tails?
Lizard eyes, octopus?
    Or slimy snails?

What's a kid to do?
    Just wait and pray.
YES! YES! YES! YES! YES!
    It's PIZZA day.

Illustrated by _____ *Date* _____

After School Today

After school today
I think I'll take a
Rocket ship to Mars.

After school today
I think I'll become a bird
And fly far away and
Never ever come back

After school today
I think I will
Take a s l o w
Boat to China.

After School today
I have
To go
To the dentist!!!

Illustrated by _____ *Date* _____

Daydreams

The boy in the back row
    sat
      and stared
out
    the window
watching
      the bird
on the branch
    fly
      free.

Illustrated by: _____ *Date* _____

Mr. Shoulda

i shoulda studied harder
for the social studies test.
i shoulda not lost my school bag
with my reading book in
it and my pencil case and
my eraser. i shoulda
not left my coat at the movies
or let my scarf, that nanna knit
me, blow away in the breeze. i
shoulda found my other sneaker
for gym but i couldn't and
i shoulda not tripped in gym class
or dropped the ball out on the
field during the game. i shoulda
been more careful in art and
not knocked over the bucket of
black paint or left the glue on
the teacher's seat. i shoulda not
burped in class or dropped my crazy
crayons all over the floor. i
shoulda listened when i talked,
i shoulda walked when i ran
down the hall and bumped smack into
the principal's broad back. i shoulda
woulda coulda done a lot of things
i know, but sometimes Mr. Shoulda
never lets me go and do the
things i know i shoulda woulda
coulda done if Mr. Shoulda
woulda let me.

Illustrated by _____   *Date* _____

Haikus

SUMMER

Blue, pink, yellow, gold
Happy splashes bright and bold
Shouts. Laughs. Cricket songs.

AUTUMN

Blood red maple leaf
Drifts softly through morning mist
Final curtain call.

WINTER

White crystal curtain
Masking the face of the earth
Hiding its life pulse.

SPRING

Gray sheets of warm rain
Green grass, flowers, buds pop-out
Welcome back old friends.

Illustrated by: _____ *Date*_____

Imagination

I s in all humans

M akes creativity marvelous

A nd all things possible.

G reat power to get to goals.

I am. I can. I will dream

N ew dreams

A nd

T urn people on by

I nventing, inspiring, igniting ideas

O n this planet that will make minds soar towards

N arnia and places beyond beginnings.

Illustrated by: _____ *Date* _____

My Journal

Some Journal & Poem Ideas for YOU to write about - in case you need ideas!
(Remember to use your senses: see, hear, smell, taste, feel.
Choose only ONE idea for each writing. Try to add dialogue.)

What would my life be like if I were a: snowflake, leaf, sneaker, boat, dinosaur,
kitten, horse, tree, bike, teddy bear, an eagle, the wind.

Things that could happen in Fall, Winter, Spring, Summer, Rainy days, Snowstorms.

My favorite: things, holiday, sport; food, hobby, animal,
vacation, friends, relative, pet, song.

Things that make me feel happy, sad, scared, angry, silly, lonely, loved, lovely.

Name and describe things that are
beautiful; miracles; red; blue, black; yellow; free.

School is best when .... , worst when .....

In kindergarten I....

When I'm 25 years my life will be....

The poem I always wanted to write is about....

The story I always wanted to write is....

Enjoy Writing. *Enjoy Writing.* *Enjoy Writing.* *Enjoy Writing!*

Index
Topic, page